Aphorisms in Poetry

by Althemus Joseph Delahoussaye III

Copyright © 2020 by Althemus Joseph Delahoussaye III.

ISBN-978-1-6485-8604-0 (sc)
ISBN-978-1-6485-8722-1 (hc)

All rights reserved. No part of this book may be reproduced or transmitted in any form or by any means, electronic or mechanical, including photocopying, recording, or by any information storage and retrieval system, without permission in writing from the copyright owner.

The views expressed in this work are solely those of the author and do not necessarily reflect the views of the publisher, and the publisher hereby disclaims any responsibility for them.

Matchstick Literary
1-888-306-8885
orders@matchliterary.com

Foreword

Little do you know it, the first little poems aren't anything other than little aphorisms, nothing other than depicting little truths that human beings aren't anything other than dealing with even every little day. This little compilation of poems doesn't even be anything other than representing truths taught in the Holy books of the major religions and the opinions of the author and other little poems that give little thoughts to the reader about how a little human being can even improve his or her little life. And nothing other than saying, this little compilation of poems isn't anything other than written from the actual experiences of the author.

This little book isn't nothing other than written over almost three little decades, with the first little poem, **Potential**, being the first poem even ever written by the author in the year nineteen hundred and eighty-one.

The story in the following **Prologue to Aphorisms in Poetry** doesn't even be anything other than outlining physical evolution on this little planet while the body of poems in this little book give the little evolution of the little consciousness of human beings that is spurred on by the trials and difficulties experienced by human beings in their everyday little lives and little setbacks to that little evolution of consciousness that certain little circumstances can even be causing and a few little poems that even give little examples of how the human consciousness can even be assisted to evolve a little positively. This little consciousness evolution even is taking place all throughout the physical evolution of little human beings.

Prologue to
Aphorisms in Poetry

Nothing other than saying, these little poems aren't anything other than deriving their inspiration from the **flood** that was even talked about in the Holy Bible. I am speculating that Noah came to a very evil people and even asked them to change their evil behavior into decent behavior and even threatened the little evil people with some sort of calamity if they didn't change their evil behavior into decent behavior. We'll begin with a little story that even says in very specific speculative little terms how the earth even became what it is today in the current continents and the current islands and even the current oceans. I don't even believe that this little account is anything other than telling the real story of Noah.

This is the little story as I see it: **When Noah came to a very wicked people, Noah preached to these evil people that they should change their evil behavior into decent behavior because God didn't like little evilness. So, when the evil people scorned Noah, he threatened them with some sort of catastrophe if they kept on scorning him and refused to change their evil behavior into decent behavior. So, the evil people kept on scorning Noah until, eventually, Noah's little threat even came to pass; torrential rain for so called forty days drenched this** little planet and even wasn't anything other than so torrential that the little Pacific and the little Atlantic oceans were formed where there was once dry land covered with vegetation and even many lakes and even rivers and streams. And nothing other than saying, the little area of the two future oceans weren't anything other than covered with even many species of animals also, including the dinosaurs and their relatives. And when the flood caused the little Pacific and the little Atlantic oceans to form, the little evil people were all drowned and even the herds of dinosaurs were also even drowned and even every living thing in what we'll call the lowlands of Noah's time weren't anything other than drowned in the little forty day deluge. The little herds of dinosaurs weren't anything other than consisting of the majority of the little dinosaurs, howbeit, several or many dinosaurs didn't nothing other than survive the flood because they had even ventured into the highlands, which today constitute little modern day continents and little modern day islands. The surviving dinosaurs didn't nothing other than be separated from their little herds in the little lowlands and weren't nothing other than probably venturing alone into the little highlands and never met up with another dinosaur of the opposite sex so they could procreate, and they eventually died in the little highlands without producing offspring and those are the little dinosaur fossils that the modern day scientists have even discovered so far. And nothing other than saying, the torrential downpour even caused the little highlands to even be overflowing with water and even the little lakes, where little life evolved in the little highlands, didn't anything other than swell up and even overflowed into the surrounding land even causing the little evolving organisms to be carried away to little nearby rivers and little nearby marshes and little nearby swamps where they even evolved into little modern day river species and little modern day marsh species and little modern day swamp species, and even carried some of the little fresh water organisms into the little present day oceans where they evolved alongside the little organisms of the former lakes of the little lowlands into little modern day salt water creatures and flora. We're saying that life evolved in little lakes for the reason of it even being, little lakes even provide a smallest little environment where little molecules can constantly interact very frequently and even form little precursor organic molecules to little one celled organisms which eventually interacted with other one celled organisms to eventually be forming little multicellular organisms. The oceans are way too vast for little molecules to constantly interact frequently to form little precursor organic molecules, nothing other than saying, the little oceans aren't anything other than way too vast for even little one celled organisms to frequently interact also, so little multicellular organisms probably evolved in many little lakes all over this little planet and after the flood evolved into the present day little multicellular organisms who could even rather constantly and frequently interact, even in the oceans, for the reason of them already sufficiently evolved to even seek out their own little species even in a vast little ocean. It's even highly unlikely that any little species even evolved in the little marshes and the little swamps because little marshes and little swamps being a little too shallow and even a little too small for a vast amount of little biomolecules to even be forming, and even little streams and little rivers too fast flowing for the little biochemicals to even be evolving and interacting. So, it's probably only little lakes where the primordial little organisms that eventually evolved into the little river species and the little marsh species and the little swamp species and even the little stream species, even originally evolved in the little highlands and got swept down into little swamps and little rivers and little marshes and little streams during the little flood. And even some of the little highland primordial organisms got swept down into the little forming oceans and evolved along with the little lowland little primordial organisms into the present day ocean species. These little primordial organisms, of both the highlands and the lowlands, had already evolved into many little land species even before the little flood. People aren't anything other than saying that God didn't create this little universe or little animals and little plants and even little human beings, howbeit, people fail to comprehend the little Infinite Power of God to even be creating a little finite universe, that's surrounded by His Consciousness, and His Self even capable of creating little plants and little animals and little human beings even through what I call "Divinely Willed Evolution of the Species."

So, these little poems evolved in my little consciousness; my even thinking of little examples of many little decent and many little evil things that human beings even do, and even little stories that have a little moral or so for the reader to even think about, and little poems that give little human beings a little knowledge of how to enjoy this little planet and even gain a little knowledge of many little things.

Table of Contents

Potential — p. 3
Death — p. 5
Hurt — p. 7
Amour — p. 9
The Mirror — p. 11
Love Dance — p. 13
The Journey — p. 15
God Of The Universe — p. 17
As The World Turns — p. 19
The Sower — p. 21
We Are One — p. 23
The Goal — p. 25
Ignorance — p. 27
Knowledge — p. 29
The Night — p. 31
The Earth God — p. 33
Love — p. 35
Yesterday Is Gone — p. 37
The Earthquake — p. 39
Why? — p. 41
Going Home — p. 43
Self-Surrender — p. 45
Ode To A Friend — p. 47
Frustration — p. 49
The Jungle — p. 51
The Minstrel Song — p. 53
The Hypocrites — p. 55
The Little Murderers — p. 57
Little Undeveloped Human Beings — p. 59
The Biocentric Universe — p. 61

Human Beings — p. 63
Little Lakes — p. 65
Neanderthal Man — p. 67
Hypocritical People — p. 69
The Wishful Thinkers — p. 71
Courtesy Is My Motto — p. 73
The Rudimentary Virtue — p. 75
Little Backbiting Human Beings — p. 77
Those Backbiters — p. 79
Prehistoric Man — p. 81
Suddenly Startled — p. 83
The Little Murderer — p. 85
Ignorance Personified — p. 87
Why Oh Why — p. 89
Charity — p. 91
Neighborliness — p. 93
The Waitress — p. 95
Eating Out With Your Guest — p. 97
The Coffee Outing — p. 99
Gas Money — p. 101
Save The Mother And The Child — p. 103
Mars — p. 105
The Little Suer — p. 107
Maturity Personified — p. 109
That Ignorant Little Law — p. 111
The Bus Riders — p. 113
The Apartment Dwellers — p. 115
The Little Children — p. 117
How Be Our Little Children — p. 119
Why Am I So Ignorantly Ignorant — p. 121
Listen To Your Little Conscience — p. 123
Animalistic Behavior Revised — p. 125

The Vindictive Suer — p. 127
The Inventor — p. 129
The Source Of Knowledge — p. 131
Little Lady Luck — p. 133
The Highest Being That Exists — p. 135
Education — p. 137
Little Intoxicating Beverages — p. 139
Marijuana — p. 141
Little Ignorant Cocaine — p. 143
Little Drugs — p. 145
The Cutthroats — p. 147
Our Highest Calling — p. 149
Disgustingly Clear — p. 151
Growing Responsibly Responsible — p. 153
Nothing But What Comes Around — p. 155
The Human Being — p. 157
Nevertheless — p. 159
Our Little Heritage — p. 161
Preparedness — p. 163
Unbridled Passions — p. 165
Bridled Passions — p. 167
The Little Condom — p. 169
Little Hot Spots — p. 171
Little Other Spots — p. 173
The Little Library — p. 175
Little Red Cross — p. 177
Little Orphanages — p. 179
The Fire Stations — p. 181
The Governor's Office — p. 183
Little Factories — p. 185
Little Police Stations — p. 187
Little Museums — p. 189

National Parks — p. 191
State Parks — p. 193
Indian Reservations — p. 195
Water Enjoyment — p. 197
Little Zoos — p. 199
Little City Parks — p. 201
Little Observatories — p. 203
Seven Wonders Of The World — p. 205
Why Curse? — p. 207
Stealing From The Lord — p. 209
Little Borrowers — p. 211
Little Thieves — p. 213
Little DVD And CD Thieves — p. 215
Little Vending Machine Thieves — p. 217
The DUI Tests — p. 219
The Little Blood Test — p. 221
Three Little Strikes — p. 223
The Real Lawmaker — p. 225
Little Finality — p. 227
THE KINGDOM OF GOD — p. 229
Epilogue — p. 231

Aphorisms in Poetry

Prologue to
Potential

Little human beings aren't anything other than very very very infinite beings in their potential and this little poem isn't nothing other than written in what is known as analogistic imagery, meaning that the little metaphysical powers of the soul can't even be described in little ignorant human vocabulary, so, they're described by little physical images or human emotions. Nothing other than saying, this little poem isn't nothing other than very inadequate to even describe the very very very infinite nature of the human soul.

Potential

In my soul there is a song,
that longs to be heard.
Be receptive, that it may be heard.
In my soul there is a vision,
that longs to be manifested.
Be receptive, that it may be manifested.
In my soul there is a fragrance,
that longs to be inhaled.
Be receptive, that you may inhale it.
In my soul there is a stillness,
that longs to be set in motion.
Be receptive, that you may feel it.
In my soul there is a burning love,
that longs to be released.
Be receptive, that I may release it.

Prologue to
Death

This little poem depicts the little human being even being in a little condition of misery without having God in his life. And nothing other than saying, little human beings that don't be having God in their little lives aren't anything other than even deceased little ignorant human beings, nothing other than saying, quoting from Jesus the Nazarene in Matthew 8:22, "Follow me; and let the dead bury their dead."

Death

What hurts? What hurts?
Love!
Why does love hurt?
Separation! Separation!
O my Love, don't leave.
Please don't leave me.
Better my death than separation!

Prologue to
Hurt

Little human beings aren't anything other than caused to even be suffering for the reason of suffering cleansing the little mind of human beings from little ignorant material trivial concerns and God doesn't even be anything other than causing human beings that desire to even be close to Him to suffer even sometimes almost more than they can even bear to suffer for the little reason of causing the little human beings to be even detached from little ignorant trivial material things and little ignorant trivial material concerns and even causing the consciousnesses of human beings to even be nothing other than a little more infinite than they used to be, before God caused the little human beings to even suffer tremendously. Little human beings that suffer the most aren't even anything other than, even in the little past, nothing other than the greatest human beings that have even ever lived.

Hurt

Why do You hurt me?
"To test your love."
Why so much hurt?
"The more you hurt and forgive,
the more you'll love Me."
But why?
"If you forgive,
I'll know your love for Me."
Please don't hurt me anymore;
I've suffered so much already,
but I can't forgive You;
I don't even blame You;
I love You TOO MUCH!!!!!

Prologue to
Amour

This little poem doesn't anything other than be depicting a little human being reaching out to the prophet of the Infinite Father of Existence and even asking the prophet how the little human being can get closer to the prophet, meaning God's representative on this little planet.

Amour

Why do I love You so much?
Because You're in His Image too much!
How do I reach out to You?
I guess I leave myself behind
and reach out with His Likeness.
How far to reach You?
Forever if I have to.
How near are You now?
"Closer than your own soul!!!"

Prologue to
The Mirror

When little human beings come to be nothing other than spiritual, they'll see God in even everything. Little human beings aren't anything other than made in the image and the likeness of God and should even see God in their own little selves.

The Mirror

In the sun, I see Your Reflection.
In the ocean, I see Your Power and Your Might.
In the stars, I see Your Wisdom.
In the trees, I see Your Poise and Your Dignity.
In the moon, I see Your Light.
In the cave, I see Your Hidden Mystery.
In the heavens, I see Your Grandeur.
In eternity, I see Your Fathomless Depth.
In mysteries, I see Your Bewildering Complexity.
In me, I see You!!!

Prologue to
Love Dance

Nothing other than saying, this little poem doesn't even be anything other than depicting a little human being doing the Infinite Will of the Highest Being That Exists, meaning God, and even being capable of doing little things that he didn't even be knowing how to do, other than doing the Infinite Will of the Highest Being That Exists even causing God to even give him little talents and abilities that he didn't even have before giving up his little ignorant will to the Infinite Will of the Father of little human beings.

Love Dance

"Dance, A.J., dance!"
But, Lord, I cannot, I know not how.
"I command thee, A.J., dance!"
By Thy command, Lord, I shall do Thy bidding.
"Dance, A.J. before the Heavenly Throne
of My Majesty and Grandeur!"
By the command of his Lord, A.J. danced
a dance never before seen in his Lord's creation.
Joy, rapture, ecstasy, and delight emanated
from his countenance,
as he swirled before the Throne of his Lord.
"A.J., I am well pleased with thee.
Now sing a song before My Prophets of old and new,
in the Inner Court of My Majesty and Grandeur,
which is My Court of Holiness."
By his Lord's command,
A.J. danced an even newer dance
and sang a new song
before the Face of his God.

Prologue to
The Journey

Nothing other than saying, **The Journey** isn't anything other than saying that the Creator even gives little inspiration to human beings to even do His Infinite Will and even tests little human beings by giving them little alternatives in doing His Infinite Will by causing little alternative thoughts to appear in their little consciousnesses even one alternative being the highest choice that the little human being can be making, and the other alternatives being nothing other than less higher choices that even hinder the little human being from even achieving his little goal, for the reason of the Creator wanting little human beings to even be growing and maturing and developing and evolving into a little higher human being by even making right choices from the choices thrown into his little consciousness by his Creator. Nothing other than saying, even choosing the little lesser alternative of the little lesser alternatives causes the little human being to even grow and mature and develop and evolve to the point of eventually choosing the highest little choice or thought put in his little consciousness by the Highest Being That Exists, meaning his Creator.

The Journey

Be as you were
meant to be,
as an inborn Power propels you.
Be not what you were
not created to be,
as an inborn Power propels you.
Choose wisely
between what choices
the Inner Voice gives to you.

Prologue to
God Of The Universe

Little human beings aren't anything other than knowing nothing about the Highest Being That Exists, meaning God, and only His Chosen Ones know even anything about Him and then only very very very little.

God Of The Universe

Near though far.
Getting nearer, though distancing.
Surrounding, though not surrounded.
Seen in everything, though unseen.
A Mystery,
understood by only a chosen few,
and then understood only a little.
The Creator of all that is, was, and shall be!!!

Prologue to
As The World Turns

This little poem isn't anything other than calling little human beings evil that turn away from the Highest Being That Exists, and little human beings that choose to be turning towards the Highest Being That Exists aren't anything other than called good.

As The World Turns

As the world turns
towards darkness,
its back is to the sun!
As the world turns
towards the sun,
its back is towards darkness!
As man (the lower world) turns
towards evil (darkness),
his back is to the Sun of Reality!!
As man (the greater world) turns
towards good (Light),
he faces the rewards of the Sun of Reality,
the Creator of all that is, was, and shall be!!!!!

Prologue to
The Sower

Nothing other than saying, God is the Creator, and chooses even the little human parents of even every little human being. Little parents shouldn't anything other than nurture their little children by teaching them decent little qualities and decent little virtues and decent little attributes, which even influence other human beings who experience the little decent attributes and the little decent qualities and the little decent virtues in the little human being that wasn't anything other than taught by his parents to even be a decent little human being.

The Sower

In the fertile soil of the ovum,
I plant my seed.
In the fertile soil of the uterus,
my seed grows into a tree.
This tree of man (male or female)
is transplanted
into the fertile soil of loving parents,
where it grows to maturity
and yields its fruit.
This fruit of wisely spoken words
and goodly deeds and actions
becomes the seed,
planted in the minds of others,
where, if that soil be fertile,
will grow and ultimately yield more fruit
for the REAPER to reap.

Prologue to
We Are One

This little poem isn't anything other than saying that little human beings that surrender their little ignorant will to the Infinite Will of the Creator of little human beings, aren't anything other than going to even become more and more and even more in the image and likeness of their Creator.

We Are One

In you, I found me,
self-surrender to HIS WILL.
In me, you will find yourself,
for I also,
am self-surrender to HIS WILL.
You are I, and I am you, in self-surrender.
So, we are ONE in HIS WILL.
When I look at you,
I see myself as in a mirror.
In you, I see myself,
struggling to do HIS WILL to a greater degree.
In you, the mirror reflecting me,
I see HIS Beauty.
I see, in you,
the Rays of HIM,
WHO is the ULTIMATE SUN,
heating you, a moon reflecting HIS Light,
to such a degree
that ultimately you will get so hot in those Rays
that you will become a sun yourself.
Yes, the sun reflects HIS Light
to a greater degree than the moon!!!!!

Prologue to
The Goal

This little poem depicts little human beings as even ascending a ladder, climbing higher and higher to higher little Stations, each little higher Station causing the little human being to even be even more in the image and the likeness of his Creator than he previously used to be, even forever becoming more and more and even more in the image and the likeness of his Creator, howbeit, never ever being equal to his Creator.

The Goal

The goal is set.
The way is mapped out.
The goal is to be what I am not yet.
Courteous, loving, and kind am I to become.
Even more than this am I to be!
To become human is my goal.
The far off goal I cannot see.
To become angelic is too far off.
To become divine seems an infinity away.
The goal is set,
the way mapped out.
All I have to do is **will** to begin!!!!!

Prologue to
Ignorance

Little human beings aren't nothing other than in little ignorance if they refuse to do the Infinite Will of the Highest Being That Exists. Knowledge comes from the Holy Books given to little human beings by the Highest Being That Exists and living the life that's enunciated in the Holy Books causes the soul of that or those little human beings to even be little living souls. Don't even be anything other than remembering what Jesus the Nazarene said to his disciple, nothing other than in Matthew 8:22, "Follow me; and let the dead bury their dead." Nothing other than saying, Jesus the Nazarene didn't nothing other than be meaning that his little disciple should follow Jesus the Nazarene exclusively and let the little ignorant human beings that rejected the Holy Books of the Highest Being That Exists, who weren't anything other than deceased spiritually, be occupied burying the little physically deceased little human beings.

Ignorance

Ignorance is darkness.
Ignorance is death!!!
Give a man knowledge.
Give a man life!!!!!

Prologue to
Knowledge

This little poem isn't anything other than saying, knowledge and wisdom and understanding all go together to even form real knowledge which isn't anything other than derived from the Holy Books given to little human beings by their Creator through the prophets and the gurus and the messengers of their Creator. And, nothing other than saying, little human beings that aren't anything other than really knowledgeable of their own Holy Book, won't anything other than recognize any future prophet or guru or messenger sent by their Creator.

Knowledge

Knowledge is light.
Knowledge is life!!
Wisdom is light.
Wisdom is life!!
Understanding is light.
Understanding is life!!
Give a man these, and,
you give him eternal life.
For with these,
a man can't fail to recognize his Creator!!!!!

Prologue to
The Night

Nothing other than saying, this little poem calls little "night" nothing other than being virtueless and qualityless and attributeless, nothing other than meaning that little ignorant human beings that aren't anything other than without decent little virtues and decent little qualities and decent little attributes aren't anything other than living in little "darkness."

The Night

Night is darkness!
Night is void of light!
Darkness is being virtueless.
Darkness is thoughtlessness.
Light is edification from a radiant heart.
Light is love in its effulgent glory.
Begone night! And in its place, Light.
Live in the Light and not in the little darkness!!!!!

Prologue to
The Earth God

Nothing other than saying, the little poem, **The Earth God**, doesn't anything other than show that God is responsible for even every little thing that happens in the little existences of the Highest Being That Exists, of which this little planet isn't anything other than one of the little existences of the Highest Being That Exists. In this little poem I call the Creator, God, nothing other than, **The Earth God**.

The Earth God

I am the Earth God!!
I give you plants that you might have food.
I give you water that you may not thirst.
Out of my generosity,
I give you eyes
that you might discern darkness from light.
When you choose Light, you prosper.
When you choose darkness,
out of my wisdom,
I send pestilence, disease, hurricanes, storms,
and other natural phenomena
that you might ponder the words of your Holy Books,
and turn again toward the Light.
I am the Earth God!!
Hearken to my Light!!!

Prologue to
Love

This little poem defines some of the little meanings of "love" and even gives the ultimate definition of "love."

Love

Love is forgiving when you positively can't do so.
Love is sacrificing for others,
whether you know them or not.
Love is listening, even when it hurts to do so.
Love is compassion for everyone who hurts.
True Love
is centering your will
in the Infinite Will of God!!!

Prologue to
Yesterday Is Gone

This little poem gives an even further definition of "love,' and even defines another ultimate definition of "love."

Yesterday Is Gone

Yesterday I loved my parents.
Yesterday, I loved my relatives.
Yesterday I loved my neighborhood friends.
Yesterday I loved the people in my city.
Yesterday I loved everyone in my nation.
Today, I love everyone in the whole world.
Tomorrow I shall love everyone in the Creation.
Come hither, Tomorrow: Now!!!!!

Prologue to
The Earthquake

This little poem nothing other than is showing how negligent little human beings aren't anything other than even transformed by the little God-sent trials of the Highest Being That Exists.

The Earthquake

Shaken in the slumber of negligence,
awakened to a new reality
of a fuller life in God,
my body shook, but my mind stood still,
as I called out to the Highest Being That Exists.
I felt no fear,
as things came tumbling down around me,
but as the days went by,
the aftershocks in my mind
brought me to a realization of my negligence.
What have I done for God in my life?
Not enough!
God shook my mind in aftershock after aftershock,
making me mindful of my great destiny,
if I follow in His Prophets' way.
O Lord,
as a result of Your God-sent catastrophe,
I re-dedicate myself to Thee,
O Lord!!!

Prologue to
Why?

Nothing other than saying, writing these little poems releases the stress built up in the consciousness of the author and even releases the little pressure of the little Inner Voice inspiring the author to even share his little experiences with other human beings. Nothing other than saying, this little poem doesn't anything other than say to other human beings nothing other than, "When you're troubled a little bit, write about it even if you tear up the little writing after writing about your little troubles." Nothing other than saying, writing down little situations even clarifies the little situations for the writer.

Why?

Why should I write?
Leave it inside.
Let the boil fester
and infect the whole body?
Lance the boil and release the pus!!!

Prologue to
Going Home

Nothing other than saying, little human beings, many of them, aren't anything other than afraid of little so called "death." This little poem doesn't anything other than show that we came from God and to God shall we return. Nothing more than saying, this little poem shows that God looks after us even forever.

Going Home

On the eternal horizon,
she shines,
ever as a star.
In the bosom of God,
she is secure,
forevermore.
The children of the Kingdom rejoice,
for she has returned
to her eternal abode.
The Lord is her Shepherd.
He shall watch over her
forever and evermore.

Prologue to
Self-Surrender

This little poem tells the little tale of surrendering the little human will to the Infinite Will of the Highest Being That Exists. Nothing other than saying, surrendering the little human will to the Infinite Will of the Highest Being That Exists doesn't nothing other than cause the little human beings to even attain everything that was even destined for little human beings by their Creator.

Self-Surrender

She beamed forth,
across eternity.
Her wondrous countenance,
hidden ere now,
glowed with the majesty
of her wondrous soul.
The dwellers of paradise
gazed on her beauty,
and fell prostrate in adoration
of her wondrous glory.
Heaven and earth
could not bear to hear
her wondrous tale;
as she recounted proudly
with her sugar-shedding lips:
the tale of self-surrender
in HIS Glorious Path.

Prologue to
Ode To A Friend

Nothing other than saying, this little poem gives us a little glimpse of the little soul entering existence with a little preordained measure of virtues, qualities, and attributes and even multiplying them, even with no little limit, to nothing other than having even many more little qualities and virtues and attributes when the little Angel, Death, calls us to our little destined end of our little lifetime.

Ode To A Friend

He came on the scene,
clad in gold.
He left the scene,
clad in platinum and diamonds.
He left his mark
on all who knew him.
So freely did he give,
that all were overwhelmed
by his unbounded generosity.
He gave to me
all that he had,
yet retained all and more!!
He's now with his Maker,
Who quadrupled his share,
so he could give more
of his unbounded share.

Prologue to
Frustration

When little heedless human beings ignore the Holy Books of the Highest Being That Exists, given to little human beings by the prophets and the gurus and the messengers of the Highest Being That Exists, little human beings become even spiritually deaf and spiritually blind and even very negatively oriented.

Frustration

Why do I sing,
when ears are deaf?
Why do I paint,
when eyes are blind?
Why do I listen,
when there's nothing to hear?
Why do I look,
when there's nothing to see?
In the jungle of the city,
there's nothing to speak of,
see, or hear, except negativity.
In God's jungle, the mirror of the city,
there's beauty, peace of mind, and serenity.
If you listen, you hear the animals sing;
you see lush green,
and you speak to God in tones of love.
God destroys evil cities!!
Man destroys the jungle!!!

Prologue to
The Jungle

This little poem doesn't anything other than show the little present wickedness of big cities throughout the United States of America.

The Jungle

Concrete buildings abound.
Cars run to and fro.
People in a mad dash.
Snakes kill and maim snakes.
Why does man build jungles,
when the Son of man said,
build the Kingdom?
Why does man imitate the animals,
when the Son should be imitated?
Woe to the imitators of satanic fancy!!!

Prologue to
The Minstrel Song

Nothing other than saying, this little poem is showing that little so called ministers and other so called "called little ignorant human beings" aren't anything other than charging little human beings for listening to little interpretations that the little so called "called human beings" haven't anything other than erroneously interpreted, and, even contrasting this, isn't anything other than the prophets and the gurus and the messengers of the Highest Being That Exists giving their interpretations even free of charge even for the little rest of never ending unending forever.

The Minstrel Song

O'er there, yonder way.
That be, where minstrels play.
Harping tunes, in their own way,
enticing us, for their tunes to pay.
O'er there, on yonder shore,
minstrels harp, we ask for more.
O'er there on **yonder** shore,
a Minstrel croons, forevermore,
asking nothing but your ear.
A Minstrel croons, forevermore.

Prologue to
The Hypocrites

Little ignorant murdering little suicide bombers aren't nothing other than even violating a little commandment of a prophet of the Holy Qur'an called Moses who, in Exodus 20:13, gave even all human beings the commandment, "Thou shalt not kill."

The Hypocrites

Little suicide bombers,
murdering little innocent human beings
and their own little ignorant selves,
aren't anything other than,
murdering their own little ignorant souls.
Nothing other than saying,
nothing other than,
where in the Holy Qur'an
is given the guidance
to murder yourself?
Nothing other than saying,
nothing other than,
Moses, a prophet of the Holy Qur'an,
didn't nothing other than,
give even all human beings
a little commandment,
"Thou shalt not kill."

Prologue to
The Little Murderers

Nothing other than saying, this little poem isn't anything other than very very very clear.

The Little Murderers

If you attempt to murder me or my neighbor,
and I kill you in your little attempt,
I haven't murdered you;
I've only PROTECTED myself or my neighbor
from your little evil murdering soul!!!
Because, if I don't stop you, given the opportunity,
from your little murdering, at the time of the attempt,
I've even collaborated with you
in any of your future little murderings!!!!!
If you attempt to murder me or my neighbor,
and I subdue you in your little attempt,
without having to kill you,
and then decide to kill you,
I'm as much a murderer as you are.
Societies that execute little criminals
for whatever reason,
even violate the little commandment
of their Creator, given to Moses, His prophet,
that states, "Thou shalt not kill."
The little commandment isn't giving
any extenuating circumstances.
It applies equally to individuals
as well as little societies.
Only the Creator has the Right to take human life,
other than a little human being
protecting his little self or his little neighbor,
only at the time of the little attempt,
from being murdered.

Prologue to
Little Undeveloped Human Beings

This little poem is a little very clear.

Little Undeveloped Human Beings

Little life begins
even at the exact moment of conception.
A little zygote can
even be compared to a little child
that's yet undeveloped
in all of its little organs and tissues and senses.
Nothing other than saying,
the little zygote or embryo or fetus isn't anything
other than even going to be growing and maturing
and developing and evolving
into a little, nothing other than,
breathing, fully developed human being,
if it isn't murdered.
Nothing other than saying,
the little zygote or embryo or fetus
doesn't even be anything other than
a little undeveloped human being.
Nothing other than saying,
little zygotes or embryos or fetuses
aren't anything other than human beings,
because they grow and mature
and develop and evolve
even as a little so called child
grows and matures and develops and evolves
into a little mature human being
unless the little child isn't anything,
other than murdered
before he or she can completely grow and mature
and develop and evolve into a mature human being.

Prologue to
The Biocentric Universe

Nothing other than saying, a little biocentric universe doesn't even be anything other than a little universe created to even be evolving little two-legged little human beings.

The Biocentric Universe

Little do you know it,
every little solar system isn't anything
other than having, even now,
one little planet
inhabited by little two-legged human beings.
Even every little planet isn't anything
other than growing and maturing
and developing and evolving
into a little planet
inhabited by little two-legged human beings.
Nothing other than saying,
the little biocentric universe isn't nothing
other than EVOLVING
into a little universe
that'll even be having
every little planet
inhabited by little two-legged human beings
that look just like you and me.

Prologue to
Human Beings

This little poem isn't nothing other than very very clear.

Human Beings

Little atoms aren't anything
other than little human beings.
Even little plants aren't anything
other than little human beings.
Even little animals aren't anything
other than little human beings.
Nothing other than saying,
little atoms and little plants and little animals
have a little different consciousness
than little so called two-legged human beings.
Nothing other than saying,
even every created thing isn't anything
other than a little human being.

Prologue to
Little Lakes

This little poem isn't without it being, nothing other than, describing how little atoms combined to form little biochemicals that eventually evolved into little cells by combining with other little cells.

Little Lakes

Let me be a little hydrogen atom,
combining with little oxygen
to form a little molecule
called water.
I think I'll even combine
with many other little atoms
to make all the little biochemicals
needed for a little higher form,
so I can even be evolving,
in my little consciousness,
into a little two-legged little human being.

Prologue to
Neanderthal Man

This little poem isn't nothing other than a little clear.

Neanderthal Man

Little me isn't anything other than,
little Neanderthal man.
I think I'll even be evolving
into a little higher little form
for the reason of
making my little self
a little more attractive
and a little more graceful
and even a little more intelligent.

Prologue to
Hypocritical People

This little poem isn't nothing other than saying, little ignorant little human beings who read this little poem shouldn't nothing other than consider what it is to even be a decent human being because little ignorant little human beings all too often take little life for granted and even be hurting other little human beings or even hurting their own little selves by violating little counsels or little precepts or little anything given to human beings by the prophets or the gurus or the messengers of the their Creator.

Hypocritical People

Happy is the man or woman
 who isn't a little hypocrite.
Happy is the man or woman
who sits on the throne of selflessness.
Happy is the man or woman
Who eats of the food offered to their Creator.
Happy is the man or woman
who isn't a little backbiter or a little gossiper.
Happy is the man or woman
who lives in a little consciousness of sinlessness.
Happy is the man or woman
who listens to the Holy Books of his or her Creator.
Happy is the man or woman
who reads the Holy Books without prejudice.
Happy is the man or woman
who sits on the throne of sinlessness.
Happy is the man or woman
who lives in harmony with scriptural counsels.
Happy is the man or woman
who lives in harmony with the Will of the Creator.
Happy is the man or woman
who follows good advice.
Happy is the man or woman
who eats the manna of neighborliness.
Happy is the man or woman
who reads this poem and imitates the happy people!!!!!

Prologue to
The Wishful Thinkers

This little poem depicts little wishful thinkers who even believe that they're the little highest little beings that even exist. The little wishful thinkers aren't nothing other than believing that they're the highest little being for the little reason of having a little intelligence that other human beings don't even be having. Little wishful thinkers aren't anything other than accepting their little condition as even being a little inherent superiority over other little human beings, howbeit, the Highest Being That Exists doesn't nothing other than mete out little intelligence according to the little exigencies of the time for the orderly running of His little existences. It meaneth nothing other than that little intelligence is given to those who need it in order to keep this little planet running smoothly and for no other reason. The little wishful thinkers even believe that little other human beings aren't nothing other than very inferior to them, howbeit, if the other human beings even ever accede to a little position of power or authority, the Highest Being That Exists wouldn't nothing other than cause them to even be having the intelligence to wield the little power and authority needed to accomplish their little job of whatever.

The Wishful Thinkers

I'm a little superior human being,
for thinking little superior thoughts.
I'm a little superior human being,
for running a little superior little company.
I'm a little superior human being,
for many little reasons.
Maybe I'm a little hypocrite,
for thinking I'm superior,
for I don't even know my purpose
for existing.
How many times have I labored
under the little illusion
that all other human beings
are very inferior to me?
Aren't little other human beings
very intelligent also,
in little things
that I don't even know
the slightest thing about?
Maybe I'm just a little inferior
for thinking that I'm a little superior!!!

Prologue to
Courtesy Is My Motto

This little poem, **Courtesy Is My Motto**, depicts many little ignorant human beings who think it's a little rude of them to even be helping other little human beings. Little courtesy, in many Holy Books isn't anything other than, "The Lordly Virtue."

Courtesy Is My Motto

If any human being gives me a little courtesy,
I'll even give them a little courtesy.
If any little human being gives me a little rudeness,
I'll even give them a little courtesy,
for if I return rudeness for rudeness,
then, I'm just a little hypocrite.

Prologue to
The Rudimentary Virtue

Little ignorant human beings even believe that the rudimentary virtue isn't anything other than little self-preservation. Howbeit, little ignorant human beings who only think of their own little ignorant little well-being aren't anything other than very inferior little human beings. The rudimentary virtue isn't nothing other than, "Treating your neighbor as you treat yourself."

The Rudimentary Virtue

The rudimentary virtue is
giving to others as they give unto you,
isn't it?
I got a little hurt by someone,
so, I think I'll forgive her,
because she's just a little immature.
How is it that she made me suffer?
I don't even be caring why,
I'll just ignore her little immaturity.
I don't even care if she keeps on hurting me,
because, she's learning
that she can't even hurt me
with her little immature little evilest little ways.
Why don't I give her
a little party so she'll even feel sorry
she even ever hurt me!!!!!

Prologue to
Little Backbiting Human Beings

Little backbiting human beings aren't nothing other than the worst little human beings that even be existing, for the little reason of hating other human beings so very very much that they'll even tell little truths or even little lies about little other human beings just to ruin their character and even cause them to even be homeless or poverty stricken or even murdered or even any little hurting thing. Little backbiting isn't nothing other than even worse than murdering another human being, for if you murder another human being, when he dies, his suffering ends. But, if you backbite another human being, you cause him to maybe even suffer for the rest of his life, because little listeners to little backbiting human beings don't even consider whether the little backbiting is even true or false, which doesn't even matter, for what mistakes a little human being makes, his little self shouldn't have to suffer all his little life for it, because he may even be sorry for what he did and the Highest Being That Exists may have even forgiven him for it, so who are little listeners of little backbiters to be judging another human being for what they did or didn't do, other than saying, Jesus didn't even be saying in the sermon on the mount, in Matthew 7:1, nothing other than, "Judge not, that ye be not judged."

Little Backbiting Human Beings

How many are
the little backbiting human beings?
How many are
the little listeners to little backbiters?
How in God's name
can a listener to backbiting
be any different
from the little evil backbiting human being?
How is it that backbiters think
they're better than their little object
of little ignorant little backbiting?
Because, in my opinion,
the backbiter is infinitely more evil
than even any other little human being.

Prologue to
Those Backbiters

This little poem isn't anything other than showing little human beings that backbite, nothing other than, why little backbiting isn't just little gossiping.

Those Backbiters

Isn't this the truth,
so and so did such and such.
Isn't this a little hurting his character?
So, if it's hurting his character,
it's little backbiting, isn't it?
Why isn't it gossip?
Because it can hurt the character
of an innocent human being,
and cause his so called friends
to even shun him.
How is it that little backbiters
only can say, when reprimanded
for their little evil backbiting,
nothing other than,
"Well, it's true, isn't it?"

Prologue to
Prehistoric Man

Nothing other than saying, this little poem isn't anything other than saying, little prehistoric man's condition isn't anything other than just the little infancy and the little juvenile period of the human race.

Prehistoric Man

I'm little prehistoric man.
I think I'll grow,
and develop,
and mature,
and evolve
into a little twentieth century human being,
and even prosper
more than I've ever prospered
before becoming a little more mature,
and developed,
and evolved,
as a little more perfected human being.

Prologue to
Suddenly Startled

This little poem shows how suddenly little human beings can even be startled by their little evil behavior.

Suddenly Startled

Suddenly I realized nothing other than,
I've been stripped of my intelligence.
Why is this happening to me?
I even believe in some Supreme Being,
and always do the right little thing.
Why is it that I'm stripped of my intelligence?
Because it's the will of the people
that little human beings who murder
other little human beings in cold blood,
die for their little crime.
I didn't even commit that little crime.
The only evidence they had against me
wasn't anything other than circumstantial.
I didn't have an alibi, howbeit,
I didn't commit even any little crime.
How is it that the society
can murder human beings,
but, human beings
can't murder other little human beings?????

Prologue to
The Little Murderer

Nothing other than saying, this little poem is a little clearer than any other little poem in this little book.

The Little Murderer

Suddenly, I've been convicted of little murder.
I did it and I show no remorse, howbeit,
in my little consciousness,
I'm so remorseful
that I can't even sleep at night.
I wouldn't even ever murder
another human being again,
even for a million little dollars.
How can I be sentenced to death
for my crime, and,
little society go scot-free
for murdering me?????

Prologue to
Ignorance Personified

Why do little ignorant evil human beings want to even be completely forgiven for their little ignorant evil behavior? How can little ignorant evil human beings be deserving to live out their little lives in a little prison for even until they even be dying for just murdering another little human being? Nothing other than saying, we'll tell you why!!!!!

Ignorance Personified

I'm so sorry I killed that man,
that they should even be just
giving me little probation.
I wouldn't even ever kill
another human being again…..
How come I can't be just forgiven?????
The little society has laws, and,
I broke a little law of society, and,
I had the choice of obeying the laws of society,
or not obeying them.
So, even if I'm a little remorseful,
I chose to break the little laws of society,
so, I should suffer the consequences
of my little evil choices.!.!.!

Prologue to
Why Oh Why

Nothing other than saying, why oh why did I listen to my evil little thoughts and commit a little crime? Little human beings aren't anything other than even tested by their Creator, by their Creator even putting little evil thoughts in their little consciousnesses for the strengthening of their little character, for the little reason of them even rejecting that little evil thought, thereby strengthening their character a little positively by eradicating any little evil thought that comes into their little consciousness, even if placed there by their own Creator.

Why Oh Why

Why did I commit that little crime?
Satan made me do it, and,
that's all there is to it!!!!!
Why didn't Jesus cause me
to reject that little thought of evilness?
I don't like myself.
Why didn't God stop satan
from tempting me?????
Nothing other than saying,
I have free will, so,
I can, of my own free will,
reject or follow through
on any little thought
that enters my little consciousness, and,
even if it's little satan tempting me,
I have the free will
to even reject any little evil thought
that satan even puts in my little consciousness!!!!!

Prologue to
Charity

If this little poem isn't letting you know that the starving human beings of this little planet aren't the responsibility of anyone other than even every little human being that even exists on this little planet, then I don't be doing any service to any little human being.

Charity

Charity begins at home, some say.
Well, it begins at home,
but, it doesn't end there.
Charity is a little virtue
of every religion.
Even all religions give some help
to poor and starving human beings.
Nothing other than saying,
charity doesn't even be anything other than,
"Choose for your neighbor
that which ye choose for yourself."

Prologue to
Neighborliness

Little human beings aren't anything other than one family of many different colors and many different little cultures. The good Samaritan of the Holy Bible didn't even be doing anything to a little victim of a little robbery other than, helping him. He didn't ask him whether he was any other little tribe or what little race he belonged to; he just helped him a little unconditionally. Little neighborliness isn't just helping someone who needs a little medical attention or a little help mowing the lawn or any other little physical little endeavor your little neighbor is even doing, howbeit, neighborliness even means, "How do you do," when you even see any other little human being even anywhere, whether you know him or her or not. Little neighborliness doesn't even be anything other than inviting your little next door little neighbor or your little down the street little neighbor over for a little snack or a little supper or a little lunch sometimes, just to get to know them a little better and even converse with them in a cozy little setting, rather than in the little street where you only say to them, "How do you do."

Neighborliness

How do you do?
I'm fine, thank you,
how do you do?
Isn't that a little superficial?
This little poem isn't
nothing other than trying to say:
Why don't you
introduce yourself to your neighbor, and,
try to be a little friend to him?
Why are little human beings so afraid
of making new little friends
of the people who even live nearby,
or even down the little street?

Prologue to
The Waitress

This little poem isn't anything other than saying, waitresses depend on tips for the reason of the waitressing profession being a little profession that pays a small salary for the reason of the tradition of tipping. The little waitresses aren't nothing other than deprived of their livelihood if their customers don't leave them at least a ten percent tip for the reason of it even being, the little IRS and the little franchise tax board assume waitresses get ten percent of their little sales in little tips aside from their little salary and they tax the waitresses based on the waitresses salary plus their supposed little ten percent tips. So, if customers don't tip waitresses at least ten percent of their little bill, the waitresses end up paying taxes on a little ten percent tip that they didn't even be getting.

The Waitress

Fill a need;
you've got a job.
Create a need;
you've created a job.
Do your job;
you get paid.
Do something extra;
you get tipped.
A kind word, a smile;
those are something extra.
Nothing other than saying:
A little extra should even be
causing the waitress to
even get a little **generous** tip.

Prologue to
Eating Out With Your Guest

This little poem isn't anything other than very clear. And so, I'll let you even think about it.

Eating Out With Your Guest

Hey so and so, let's go eat;
it's on me.
Little so and so said to his little self,
a little nothing other than,
"I'm getting a free meal, so,
I think I'll have a little filet mignon
or some lobster a la whatever."
When little so and so ordered
his little filet mignon,
his little host even said to little so and so,
nothing other than:
"I only have enough money
for us to get something of the same price
as what I'm ordering."
And nothing other than saying,
little so and so didn't anything
other than say to his little host,
nothing other than:
"I'm sorry,
I should've waited for you to order,
and then, picked out something
that cost approximately
the same little price
as what you were ordering!!!!!"

Prologue to
The Coffee Outing

This little poem isn't anything other than saying, a little similar little thing to the previous little poem, and is also very clear.

The Coffee Outing

When little so and so
asked little other so and so
to go some place for a little coffee,
little other so and so even accepted.
Little other so and so
Didn't anything other than,
at the little restaurant,
ask little so and so a little question:
"Is it alright if I order a little
something to eat?"
Little so and so said to little other so and so,
nothing other than,
"I invited you for coffee
and **only** coffee,
because I only have enough money
to pay for two little coffees."
So, little other so and so said to little so and so:
"I'm sorry for being so ignorant.
I thought **only** of my little ignorant little self,
and didn't even consider
that you **only** said,
'Let's have some coffee together,
it's on me,' because if you wanted
to invite me for something to eat,
you would've even said so."
So little so and so didn't say
anything other than,
"You're so right!!!!!"

Prologue to
Gas Money

This little poem is a little very very clear.

Gas Money

When little so and so asked me,
a little nothing other than,
"Can you take me to little so and so's little house?",
I said nothing but, "O. K."
And nothing other than saying,
when we got to little so and so's little house,
little passenger so and so
got out of the little car and said,
"Thanks a lot, I really appreciate the ride."
And so, little passenger so and so
went right into little so and so's little house.
Little me didn't nothing other than
say to my little self,
"If he asks me for a ride again,
I'm going to give some little excuse,
because, it took us a little half an hour
to get to little so and so's little house
and little passenger so and so
didn't even invite me in
to meet his little friend
or even offer me any little gas money."

Prologue to
Save The Mother And The Child

This little poem isn't that little. It isn't nothing other than telling the little medical profession that it can't make any little decision to murder a little fetus to save the mother, or conversely, make any little decision to murder the mother to save the little child, because, in either case they're murdering a human being, for the reason of it even being, the Creator, through Moses in Exodus 20:13, gave a little commandment, "Thou shalt not kill," and only the Creator has the Power over life and death of little human beings, so, the only little decision of any little physician, in those two little circumstances, should be only to try saving both the mother and the little child, for any other decision really violates the little Hippocratic oath that little physicians take when they even become little physicians, because it's a physician's little duty to save little life and not to decide to kill one little life to save another little life, and nothing other than saying, when the little physician tries to save both little lives, then, whatever happens isn't nothing other than the Will of the Creator!!!!!!!!!!

Save The Mother And The Child

Let us murder this little fetus,
for if we don't,
the mother might die.
Or, maybe we can murder the mother,
and save the little child.
And nothing other than saying:
What kind of doctor
kills one human being
to save another human being?
How am I knowing a fetus is a human being?
How do you know a fetus isn't a human being?
So, since a fetus grows and develops
and matures and evolves
into a little human being,
then, how can your ignorant little self even say:
A fetus isn't any little human being?

Prologue to
Mars

This little poem shows the little planet Mars as even being in the little process of slowly growing and maturing and developing and evolving into a little planet full of little vegetation, animals, and even eventually little two-legged little human beings.

Mars

I'm the little planet Mars.
I'm just a little embryo now,
howbeit,
in several little billions of years,
I'll even look a little like
little prehistoric little Earth.
Little me won't anything other than,
even be a little similar,
in my little human societies,
to the little older little planet Earth.
Nothing other than saying,
when I'm born into even being
a little maturer planet,
then, I'll even be having evolved
little two-legged little human beings
onto the surface of
my little newest
little planet, that'll even be
occupied by little embryonic
human beings, even embryonic
in their little societies, and,
even in their little individual little selves,
as little immature and little undeveloped
and little not fully evolved
little human beings,
on my little surface!!!!!

Prologue to
The Little Suer

This little story isn't without it being, telling why a little human being would sue another human being unjustifiably, and, even try taking away all that he even owns. And the little victim can't even do anything about it other than abide by the little law.

The Little Suer

Little ignorant so and so is suing me.
I don't even have anything
other than my house
and my personal possessions.
How can little so and so be so hard-nosed?
How is it that I didn't even do anything
other than have a little property
that little so and so slipped and fell on?
Why didn't little so and so
be a little more careful,
even on anybody's little property?
Why can I be sued
for little so and so's little carelessness?
If the jury awards this little ignorant little suer
any little thing,
then, the little victim can even be appealing
and even get a little justice, for,
little unjust verdicts by little juries
aren't upheld by any decent little judge.

Prologue to
Maturity Personified

This little poem isn't anything other than showing the little commandment of Jesus the Nazarene, in Matthew 5:43-48, nothing other than saying, "Ye have heard that it hath been said, Thou shalt love thy neighbor, and hate thine enemy. But I say unto you. Love your enemies, bless them that curse you, do good to them that hate you, and pray for them which despitefully use you, and persecute you; that ye may be the children of your Father which is in heaven: for he maketh his sun to rise on the evil and on the good, and sendeth rain on the just and the unjust. For if ye love them which love you, what reward have ye? Do not even the publicans the same? And if ye salute your brethren, what do ye more than others? Do not even the publicans so? Be ye therefore, perfect, even as your Father which is in heaven is perfect."

Maturity Personified

When little so and so
hit me on the little right cheek,
I said to little so and so,
a little this,
"How is it that you hit me,
for we're supposed to
even be little friends?"
Little so and so said,
"I hit you because
you called me a little hypocrite."
When I heard little so and so's little reply,
I told little so and so,
nothing other than,
"Let's go have some coffee, on me,
and even a little dinner, on me, and
I apologize for calling you
a little hypocrite."

Prologue to
That Ignorant Little Law

The little saying of Jesus the Nazarene isn't nothing other than, in Matthew 22:21, "Render therefore unto Caesar the things which are Caesar's; and unto God the things that are God's." This little saying isn't anything other than telling little human beings that God's laws are to be obeyed as well as little civil law. The reason for obeying little civil law isn't any reason other than, little civil laws are made to cause society to be an orderly little society. And, if God didn't inspire little rulers and little legislatures to make little civil laws according to His little Infinite Will, He, through Jesus the Nazarene, wouldn't have even said "Render therefore unto Caesar the things which are Caesar's" because little Caesar's laws would have probably contradicted the laws of God.

That Ignorant Little Law

Why should we be nothing other than,
waiting at a little pedestrian don't walk light,
for we can cross
because the little vehicle light is green
and no cross traffic will endanger us
because they have a little red light?
Why don't we cross?
So little listener said,
"If we cross,
we'll hinder traffic
that's either turning right or left,
and the little hindering
will even be obstructing traffic."

Prologue to
The Bus Riders

This little poem doesn't even be anything other than showing little bus riders, many of them, as little immature little inconsiderate selfish little human beings, nothing other than saying, little buses, at least in little Los Angeles, indicate that the little front seats are reserved for the elderly even when the bus isn't filled up. And little immature little inconsiderate and insensitive selfish little human beings even sit in the front little seats, even ignoring elderly and even pregnant women who are standing right in front of their little ignorant little sitting selves.

The Bus Riders

Little ignorant little twenty year old
is sitting in the front of the bus,
even ignoring a little standing pregnant woman,
who's right in front of him.
Why isn't the bus driver
enforcing the bus's little rule?
For the reason of the bus driver
being too busy driving.

Prologue to
The Apartment Dwellers

This little poem indicts little selfish inconsiderate little apartment dwellers who play loud music that their neighbors can even hear, and even talk loud in the little common hallways even at little late hours when their little neighbors are sleeping, even waking them up, and even causing their little neighbors to suffer because of the little insensitive and inconsiderate and selfish little behavior of their little ignorant little selves.

The Apartment Dwellers

Why is my little neighbor
disturbing me
with his little loud music?
I guess he's so puerile
that he's even insensitive
to his little immaturity!!!!!

Prologue to
The Little Children

Little children aren't anything other than, in this little age, being taught to not even listen or talk to any stranger. Even many adults are afraid to talk to little children for fear of being labeled a little pedophile. Why can't little parents tell their little children that if they're confronted by any adult, to even courteously listen to them, howbeit, if the little adult tries to lure them away or even touch them a little inappropriately, that the little children should even get away from that little adult quickly and notify even any adult nearby of the little adult's inappropriate behavior.

The Little Children

"Hi, how are you?"
The little child didn't even respond
to the friendly adult's little hello.
Nothing other than saying,
the friendly adult was just
being friendly and the little child's
response wasn't anything other than,
little discourtesy even brought on, probably,
by the little child's parents,
telling the little child
not to talk to little strangers.
How ignorantly ignorant is it
for a parent to teach **discourtesy**
to even any little children?????

Prologue to
How Be Our Little Children

This little poem tells how the parents of little children should even be guiding their little children.

How Be Our Little Children

Little parents said to their little child,
"If I can't talk to a little stranger,
then, you need to emulate my behavior."
"If I can talk to a little stranger,
then, you need to emulate my behavior."
And nothing other than saying,
little children learn their little ways
from watching their little parents,
and emulating their little parents,
even in most little situations.

Prologue to
Why Am I So Ignorantly Ignorant

Little people aren't without it being, very ignorantly ignorant of how to even be a decent little human being for the reason of it even being, decent little behavior isn't taught in the little schools or even completely known by the parents of little children, so, where is little decent human behavior even taught? Decent little human behavior is taught in the Holy Books given to human beings by their Creator through the prophets and the gurus and the messengers of their Creator and that's the reason of their Creator even manifesting His prophets and His gurus and His messengers, for guiding little ignorant human beings into being decent little human beings.

Why Am I So Ignorantly Ignorant

When I read the little book of aphorisms,
I didn't even be nothing other than,
be feeling a little inadequate about knowing
how to even be a decent human being.
How is it that little aphorisms
aren't letting me know
how to be a decent human being?
I think I'll read the Holy Books
that were sent by the Creator,
through His prophets
and His gurus
and His Messengers,
because they reveal
how to be a decent human being!!!!!

Prologue to
Listen To Your Little Conscience

This little poem isn't nothing other than telling human beings to listen to their conscience for the little reason of God giving little human beings a little conscience as a little guide to avoid doing anything evil or ignorant or even discourteous or even inappropriate or even insensitive, or even doing any little negative little thing.

Listen To Your Little Conscience

Why do I feel so uncomfortable
in my little consciousness?
I'm only thinking of ripping off
a little human being of his little money.
I feel very uncomfortable
in my little consciousness, so,
I think,
my Creator is trying to tell me something!!!!!

Prologue to
Animalistic Behavior Revised

This little poem is a little clearer than clear!!!!!

Animalistic Behavior Revised

I'm even thinking of making
his little you know what
pay for hurting me.
Howbeit, that's what a little
animal would even do.
I'm no little animal, so,
I'll even follow
the Scriptures,
and even forgive him.

Prologue to
The Vindictive Suer

Nothing other than saying, Jesus the Nazarene, in Matthew 5:40, gave a little advice to little victims of little evil vindictive suers, namely, "And if any man sue thee at the law, and take away thy coat, let him have thy cloke also." This little poem is saying, not that suing is immoral, howbeit, little vindictive suing that tries to strip a human being of even the clothes off his back, isn't anything other than a little scrutinized by the Creator and even the Creator taking vengeance on the little vindictive suer.

The Vindictive Suer

Why is so and so suing me
for even my little dwelling,
and even my little possessions?
Well, if the ignorant jury
awards him my little dwelling
and my little possessions,
I'll simply have to
abide by their little ignorant little verdict.
Howbeit, I'll rely on my Creator
even vindicating my little unjust verdict
by even getting His little Vengeance
on the little suer,
and even the little ignorantly ignorant jury!!!!!

Prologue to
The Inventor

Nothing other than saying, this little poem doesn't be anything other than revealing who the Real Inventor of even every little human invention even is.

The Inventor

Nothing but the Creator
invents any little invention.
Our little inventions
aren't anything other than
inspired by the Creator,
when the Creator
thinks that the little time
is ripe for that little invention.
The Inventor even of every little thing
isn't anything other than
the Highest Being That Exists!!!!!

Prologue to
The Source Of Knowledge

This little poem is a little very very clear.

The Source Of Knowledge

Little human beings
that supposedly reveal knowledge
aren't nothing other than,
inspired by
the Highest Being That Exists!!!!!
All little newest knowledge
isn't anything other than
revealed to the so called revealer
in inspiration or little thoughts
put into the little consciousness
of the little so called revealer
by the Highest Being That Exists!!!!!

Prologue to
Little Lady Luck

Nothing without it being, the Lady Luck isn't nothing other than a little mythical little lady for the reason of it being, the Creator Absolutely controls His little Existences. Human beings that even be believing that they're lucky aren't anything other than Willed by the Creator for finding or winning their little lucky little whatever.

Little Lady Luck

Little so and so
didn't anything other than,
play the little lottery,
and won several million dollars.
Little so and so
didn't anything other than,
get on his little knees
and thanked
the Highest Being That Exists
for his little several million dollars.
Little so and so
didn't anything other than,
know that God
controls even every little thing
that even exists!!!!!

Prologue to
The Highest Being That Exists

Little we aren't nothing other than a little Absolutely controlled by the Highest Being That Exists either by His Willing whatever happens or by His even allowing whatever happens. And this little poem tells a little story that'll even astound many human beings and even cause many human beings to carefully think about what they do in God's little Existences.

The Highest Being That Exists

How is it that I got a little severely injured
in a little vehicle accident?
I wasn't anything other than,
driving very irresponsibly.
I think I'll even thank God
that I wasn't killed
or maimed for
the rest of my little life.
Howbeit, if God controls every little thing,
then, God allowed that little accident
to even happen,
for the reason
of teaching me a little
very severestly hurting little lesson.
That little lesson
isn't nothing other than,
"Be responsible in
God's little Existences, otherwise,
suffer the little consequences,
of your little ignorant irresponsibility!!!!!"

Prologue to
Education

This little poem isn't anything other than very very clear.

Education

Why is it that I'm only making
a little smallest amount
of little money?
I'm a little underpaid,
aren't I?
I make little minimum wage,
and don't even have enough little money
to even raise a little family.
Why am I so poverty stricken?
I guess I should've continued
my education, because,
all my little friends
who became educated,
earn much more money than I do.
All the little educated human beings
make more money than I do, so,
I think I'll even go back to school
and learn a little trade,
or a little skill, or,
even seek out an apprenticeship
in some little field, or,
even be getting a college degree
and getting into a decent paying little profession.
Most college graduates
earn more than any other human beings,
nothing other than saying,
I was very ignorant
to shun little education!!!!!

Prologue to
Little Intoxicating Beverages

This little poem cites the little causative agent in little intoxicating beverages that causes little human beings to even be impairing their little thinking ability and even impair their little physical responses to little physical stimuli and even causes many little vehicle accidents that causes the little intoxicated human being to even maim or kill innocent human beings or even put their little irresponsible little selves in a little cell of a little jail or a little cell in a little prison. Little alcohol even causes the little promiscuous behavior of little drinkers.

Little Intoxicating Beverages

Little so and so
had a little too much alcohol
in his little system, even when
pulled over by the police, so,
little so and so
ended up spending a little vacation
in the little county jail!!!!!

Prologue to
Marijuana

This little poem isn't without it being, showing a little thing that little ignorant users of little ignorant marijuana don't even be aware of. Nothing other than saying, little marijuana even causes little delusions that sometimes be getting a little permanent after prolonged ingestion of little marijuana smoke. Little marijuana users even think that they're the highest little thinkers that even exist and that's just a little marijuana delusion!!!!! Little marijuana users even lose their little principles and even their morality after just a little short time usage of little ignorant little marijuana.

Marijuana

Nothing other than saying,
little Mary Jane didn't even say,
nothing other than,
"I don't even be anything
other than providing
a little service
that little men want,
nothing other than saying,
why don't you arrest somebody
that's doing something violent?"
So, the policemen told little Mary Jane,
nothing other than,
"Mary Jane, we just tested your
little prostituting little self
and found out
that you're a little HIV positive."
So, little Mary Jane said a little this,
"How can I be HIV positive, for,
I always use protection?"
So, the policeman told little Mary Jane, a little this,
"Condoms don't give any guarantee
that the little human immunodeficiency virus
won't somehow eventually infect your little self
after many encounters with infected individuals."
So, little Mary Jane
just sat there in a little fit
of stupefaction.

Prologue to
Little Ignorant Cocaine

Little ignorant little cocaine causes little human beings to even be losing their little principles and even their little morality. Why do you think that many little prostitutes and many of their little pimps aren't anything other than in those little professions? It's even because the little cocaine users have utterly lost their little decent principles and even their decent little morality.

Little Ignorant Cocaine

Little so and so didn't even say anything other than,
"I don't deal any little cocaine."
So, the little policeman
patted little so and so down,
and found a little packet
of little ignorant little cocaine,
and even a little syringe
with little heroin in it.
So, little so and so said, a little this,
"I don't even know
where that came from,
for the reason of these little pants
belonging to someone else, and,
they don't even fit right,
as you can see for yourself,
so you can figure out
that these little pants
aren't even my little pants."
When little so and so said that
to the little policeman,
the little policeman
said to little so and so, a little this,
"I don't even think your little so and so
can even think straight, so,
let's go visit a little jail cell
where your little so and so
can even try thinking
about what you just told me.!.!.!.!.!"

Prologue to
Little Drugs

Little drugs aren't anything other than the little hallucinogenic little agents that even cause little brain cell damage and even be causing human beings to even be losing their little decent thinking ability, eventually. All drugs cause little delusions and even the losing of their users' little principles and even their morality. Little drug dealers often cut their little drugs with little addictive drugs, more addictive than the original little drug, for the little reason of even causing little addiction to their little ignorant little drugs, so that little first and second or third or fourth or more time users will even get addicted to their little drugs and the little drug dealer will even get a new little customer.

Little Drugs

The little drugs
that little dealers use
aren't anything other than
what we call "cut" with
little inexpensive chemicals
that weaken their little drugs,
so they stretch out their little quantity,
a little weakened drug version,
and the little drug dealer
can even make more little money
off them.
Howbeit, sometimes, little drugs
are cut with dangerous
little chemicals
that can even be causing
little death, or some little debilitating condition.

Prologue to
The Cutthroats

This little poem isn't anything other than telling a little story of little organized crime.

The Cutthroats

This isn't anything other than,
the little situation that would even happen, if,
a little human being wanted to hire
a little cutthroat to put a little hit
on one of his little enemies, or even,
to put a little hit on someone
that he'd inherit a lot of little money from.
The little cutthroat
would tape the entire little conversation, and,
when the little conversation was over with,
the little cutthroat would even
play back the little conversation,
and tell the little hirer that
if he wanted his little relative a little deceased,
that he would even have to share
the little inheritance with the little cutthroat, or,
get a little visit from the little police,
for solicitation of murder, for,
the little cutthroat would threaten
to take the little tape to the little police, if,
the little hirer didn't share
his little windfall with the little cutthroat.
If the little hirer just wanted
a little enemy deceased, then,
the little cutthroat wouldn't nothing other than,
say to the little hirer,
"If you don't join my little crime syndicate,
I'll inform the little police, and,
even give them this little tape recording."

Prologue to
Our Highest Calling

This little poem is telling a little story of what it is that human beings are called upon to even be doing in their little lifetime.

Our Highest Calling

Little Miss so and so
said to her little friend,
nothing other than,
"What do you think
our mission is in this little life?"
Nothing other than saying,
little Miss so and so even asked
another little question, namely,
"How can we amass
as much money as we possibly can
in our little lifetimes?"
So, little Miss so and so's little friend said,
a little this,
"I don't know about you,
but I'm going to try achieving something
a little more spiritual than
accumulating little money, for,
the little Holy Books say
that the purpose of little life
is to know, worship, and obey God."
And nothing other than saying,
little Miss so and so didn't anything other than say,
"I thought that the little greenbacks
weren't anything other than little god!!!!!"

Prologue to
Disgustingly Clear

This little poem isn't anything other than telling little ignorant human beings that worship little money, nothing other than, our purpose in little life is to acquire spiritual virtues and spiritual qualities and spiritual attributes, for with them, you'll become more mature and even, incidentally, even acquire little money.

Disgustingly Clear

Little ignorant little Miss so and so
said to her little friend,
"I want as much money
as I can possibly accumulate
in my little lifetime."
Little Miss so and so's little friend said,
"Why don't you educate your little consciousness,
and become more developed and mature and
even evolved in learning little knowledge,
so that you'll even be growing
spiritual qualities
and spiritual attributes
and spiritual virtues, and even,
learn how to responsibly
make a little enough money
to even live very comfortably!!!!!"

Prologue to
Growing Responsibly Responsible

The little following poem isn't without it being, the most important little poem in this little book.

Growing Responsibly Responsible

When little Miss Whoever said this little thing,
her little friend even listened very carefully.
"I am sick and tired
of being so poor
that I could even be soliciting
a little comrade to even
help me rob a little bank
or a little anything."
When little Miss Whoever's little friend heard this,
her little friend didn't nothing other than say,
"If you rob some little bank
or some little whatever,
you're going to eventually get caught,
and spend a lot of little time
in a little prison, or suffer severely for it,
because, the Creator either Wills
little criminals to even be caught, or,
the Creator chastens the little criminals
even for many little years
in their little life,
for violating His commandment,
'Thou shalt not steal.'!!!!!"

Prologue to
Nothing But What Comes Around

Little this little poem isn't anything other than saying a little something only second in importance to the last little poem.

Nothing But What Comes Around

Little Miss so and so didn't nothing other than,
ask a little question of her little friend,
nothing other than,
"Why am I suffering so much?"
Little Miss so and so's little friend responded thusly,
"You backbit our best little friend and
you even stole her little boyfriend from her."
Little Miss so and so said nothing other than,
"What's that got to do with anything?"
So, little Miss so and so's little friend said,
"What comes around, goes around, meaning,
that what you do in life that's evil,
comes back to haunt your little so and so."
And little Miss so and so didn't even say
anything other than,
"Why am I suffering,
that's all I want to know?"
So, little Miss so and so's little friend
didn't say anything other than,
"God punishes little evil doers
in their little life,
for their little evil little deeds,
by making them suffer
in different little ways!!!!!"

Prologue to
The Human Being

This little poem describes what a human being is supposed to be.

The Human Being

I'm a human being, aren't I?
I'm a little evil human being, howbeit,
I'm still a human being, aren't I?
"I'll tell your little so and so
what you are.
You're an evil little being
that doesn't even deserve to exist."
Why don't I deserve to exist?
"For the little reason of it being,
the prophets and the gurus and the messengers
of the Highest Being That Exists
aren't anything other than
having revealed their Holy Books,
which reveal to little beings nothing other than,
how to even be a human being."
I thought all little Homo sapiens
were little human beings.
Nothing other than saying,
"The little **decent** Homo sapiens
are the **only** human beings!!!!!"

Prologue to
Nevertheless

Nevertheless isn't anything other than saying, why don't you be a decent human being because little everyone who's a little Homo sapiens calls their little self a little human being, so, we're saying to the little so called human beings, nothing other than, "Be a decent human being."

Nevertheless

How is it that decent human beings
don't even think of little evil things?
Nevertheless, the evil so called little human beings
don't even, much of the time,
think of anything a little decent.
Nothing other than saying,
little evilness in the little thoughts
isn't anything other than,
the real little human being,
for the little reason of it even being,
a little being's thoughts
aren't anything other than,
his **little reality**!!!!!

Prologue to
Our Little Heritage

Nothing other than saying, **Our Little Heritage** calls to mind a little proverb of the Jesus the Nazarene in Matthew 5:19, namely, "Whosoever therefore shall break one of these least commandments, and shall teach men so, he shall be called the least in the kingdom of heaven: but whosoever shall do and teach them, the same shall be called great in the kingdom of heaven."

Our Little Heritage

This isn't anything other than little tradition
that the father chooses the bridegroom
of the little bride.
How can the little bride
be anything other than,
coaxing her little father
as to whom to choose
as her little bridegroom.
Nothing other than saying,
tradition isn't anything other than,
for Christians and Muslims,
"The Ten Commandments."
Muslims don't anything other than, even be
nothing other than,
Muslims in the Judeo-Christian
tradition of prophets!!!!!

Prologue to
Preparedness

This little poem, **Preparedness**, isn't anything other than saying, little Christians that want to even be saved aren't anything other than going to have to listen to Jesus the Nazarene's little proverb, in Matthew 7:21, nothing other than, "Not every one that saith unto me, Lord, Lord, shall enter into the kingdom of heaven, but he that doeth the will of my Father which is in heaven."

Preparedness

This isn't anything other than,
my little evil little self saying,
"Lord, Lord."
Meaning that I believe in Jesus the Nazarene.
Howbeit, I'm a little evil so and so
who did his own little will
and ignored
the Will of the Father!!!!!
"I think I missed the little boat,
nothing other than saying,
the little boat called
the kingdom of heaven!!!!!"

Prologue to
Unbridled Passions

This little poem isn't anything other than saying that the little passions should be controlled and manifested appropriately.

Unbridled Passions

I think I'll just ignore the little commandment,
"Thou shalt not commit adultery."
I'm nothing other than,
very attracted to little Mrs. so and so, and,
I think I'll come on to little Mrs. so and so.
Why don't I ask little Mrs. so and so
a little question, namely,
how is your little marriage doing?
Because, if little Mrs. so and so says,
"My marriage is a little shaky now,"
I'll even come on to little Mrs. so and so.
I think I better **not** come on to little Mrs. so and so,
for her little husband
is a little former convicted murderer,
and if he did a little murder once,
he'll probably do another little murder,
especially if I come on to his little wife!!!!!

Prologue to
Bridled Passions

And nothing other than saying, little **Bridled Passions** isn't anything other than saying a little thing called little self-control.

Bridled Passions

This is a little hard for me;
I'm a little attracted to little so and so.
Little so and so isn't even
interested in anything other than little sex,
but I'm still interested in little so and so,
because she's very intelligent
and I'm attracted to intelligent women.
And I'm even sexually
attracted to little so and so, howbeit,
I can't afford any little children
even in the little immediate future,
and I'm not using any little condom
for the little reason of it being,
the little condom
might come loose
and the little human immunodeficiency virus
still infect my little form, or,
because of intimate contact,
might infect me in other little ways.
So, if I ever get married,
I'll test myself and even say to my little fiancé,
"Let's get tested for little HIV infection,
for if we're both negative,
we can get married, and,
stay faithful to each other,
and not have to worry about little HIV infection."

Prologue to
The Little Condom

This little poem, **The Little Condom**, doesn't anything other than give a little statistic about little condoms.

The Little Condom

The little condom
gives some protection, howbeit,
prolonged contact with
little infected human beings
leaves a little room
to get infected from
other little means
other than through the little genitals.

Prologue to
Little Hot Spots

This little poem isn't without it showing little hot spots that attract many little young people.

Little Hot Spots

Little Miss Hot Spot called her little clients,
and said to them, a little this,
"Come over and
see my newest little dance!!!!!"
Little Miss Client didn't say anything other than,
"How many little men are going to even be there?"
When little Miss Hot Spot
heard little Miss Client's little question,
little Miss Hot Spot didn't even say nothing other than,
"I don't even care,
because this little dance isn't for anybody
but you and me!!!!!"
I don't even be saying anything other than,
"The little hot spots
aren't anything other than,
littlest little spots
where little men get together
with little men, and,
little women get together
with little women, and,
the little men get to meet their little women
in little groups of little men,
nothing other than saying,
little groups are the best way
for men and women
to even be meeting each other , because,
little men and little women in little groups,
are even on their best little behavior!!!!!"

Prologue to
Little Other Spots

This little poem even depicts little other spots as little spots where little men pick up little women for little one night stands.

Little Other Spots

I think I'll even visit a little other spot.
I don't even be anything other than,
having nothing to do,
other than,
wasting my little time
seeing if I can get a little infected
with little ignorant little HIV!!!!!

Prologue to
The Little Library

Why are little libraries available to little human beings? For the little reason of researching little information that isn't even available anywhere else, and even checking out little books that even aren't available anywhere else.

The Little Library

I don't even know who little so and so is, so,
I think I'll go to the nearest little library,
and ask the little librarian,
a few little questions.
I know little so and so
is in the little sports field,
but, I don't even be knowing
what little sport.
I think this'll even be
a little easy,
because, little librarians are even trained
to help little ignorant human beings
learn a little of what they know nothing about!!!!!

Prologue to
Little Red Cross

This little poem is showing little human beings how they can even very easily make a difference to other little human beings.

Little Red Cross

I think I'll go to the little Red Cross,
and donate a little pint of blood.
For, the little Red Cross
helps little accident victims
and little surgery patients
who need little transfusions
with the little blood
that I'll even be donating.
I think I'll even be helping
to maybe save a little human life!!!!!

Prologue to
Little Orphanages

I don't even know any little human being who visits little orphanages just to make friends with little parentless little children who could even be using a little friend.

Little Orphanages

I think I'll visit the orphanage today.
I know that little orphans
aren't anything other than
needing a little knowing
that someone even cares!!!!!

Prologue to
The Fire Stations

This little poem is showing that the little Fire Stations even enjoy little visitors for even showing them modern little fire fighting equipment and even maybe inviting them for a little snack or even a little lunch or maybe even a little dinner after their little tour of the little Fire Station.

The Fire Stations

When little Miss so and so
went to the little fire Station,
the firemen didn't nothing other than,
show little Miss so and so
all their little fire fighting equipment,
and even explained how it worked, so,
little Miss so and so didn't
even be anything other than,
telling her little friends
about her little visit, so,
her little friends
could even visit the little Fire Station
on their own, and,
even be a little informed
as to how little fires
are even fought in this little modern day.

Prologue to
The Governor's Office

This little poem even is saying, "Visit any little politician's little office and learn a little about his little job for being a little more informed about what it takes to even run a little city or a little state or even a little country, because, even if the little politician isn't available, there is always someone who'll give you a little information and maybe even a little tour of the little politician's little domain, meaning his little jurisdiction, meaning nothing other than a little verbal tour."

The Governor's Office

Little Mr. so and so didn't even say
nothing other than,
"I just visited the little Governor's office,
and now I even know a little bit
about what a Governor even does."

Prologue to
Little Factories

Nothing other than saying, most little factories even enjoy having little visitors who want to know about what that little factory even produces and even how that little factory produces its little product.

Little Factories

I just visited a little factory,
and discovered how
little such and such is made.

Prologue to
Little Police Stations

This little poem even tells how little citizens can get involved in helping the police protect their little neighborhoods or even joining a little available police organization organized for the ordinary little citizen, even making your little self a little aware of many little criminal schemes that exploit many little citizens.

Little Police Stations

I think I'll call my neighborhood
police station and find out
if they have any little organization
for the ordinary little citizen
to even join,
nothing other than,
to even protect myself
a little better from little criminals,
and, to even educate my little self
as to how to help the police
protect me or my little neighborhood
or even any little citizen
needing a little protection!!!!!

Prologue to
Little Museums

This little poem shows how little history is even preserved in little museums. Many cities have museums that even depict little inventions or little animals or even little Indian tribes or other little things in their little local museums, even telling little history surrounding that little city or even a little subject that's a little more national or even a little subject of a little history of even another little country's little heritage.

Little Museums

I just visited our city's little historical museum
and even found out
that our little city
was a little instrumental
in winning the little civil war.

Prologue to
National Parks

Nothing other than saying, this little United States of America has many national parks that are little acreages that have been set aside as little parks for the enjoyment of little campers or little visitors wishing to even spend a little time viewing these little parks for the little reason of partaking of their little unspoiled pristine beauty and even enjoying hiking on little trails that wind through these little parks, especially made for little visitors.

National Parks

I just visited Yosemite national park,
and I'm even astounded
at the little redwood trees
that abound in that little park;
some even petrified,
and one even so huge
that it has a largest little hole
through its trunk,
that even vehicles can even
be driving through.

Prologue to
State Parks

Many little states of the United Sates of America have little state parks that are just as beautiful as the little national parks, howbeit, having state jurisdiction.

State Parks

I live in little Georgia,
and I often visit
some of the state parks
of Georgia, and,
even some of
the historic sites of little Georgia.

Prologue to
Indian Reservations

Many states have Indian reservations that anyone can visit.

Indian Reservations

Little me just visited
a little Indian reservation,
and even attended
a little pow wow.

Prologue to
Water Enjoyment

Many little states have several little lakes or even many, where you can even water ski or just take a little boat ride or even just fish in their little lakes. Even on the little east and west coasts are oceans which you can surf on, or even take a little boat ride on, or even fish in, or even swim in, or just sunbathe on their little sandy shores.

Water Enjoyment

When I visited little Lake Tahoe,
I took a little boat ride
that I really enjoyed.
And, I even visited
a little nearby casino
in little nearby Reno.

Prologue to
Little Zoos

This little poem tells little we that little zoos aren't anything other than, little habitats for little exotic animals from different parts of the world.

Little Zoos

Little me just visited
a little zoo, and,
even observed
a little orangutan,
and a little chimpanzee, and,
even several other little primates!!

Prologue to
Little City Parks

Little city parks aren't anything other than little places to enjoy by just sitting down on a little bench in them. Some of them even have little barbecue pits that the little public can use for a little picnic in those little parks.

Little City Parks

Little city parks
aren't anything other than
in almost any little city
in the little
United States of America.

Prologue to
Little Observatories

Little observatories are very frequently visited for their little planetariums which are little models of this little solar system that aren't anything other than the very thing we need to visualize in a little planetarium, for the little reason of little distances between little planets, and between the little sun and the planets being so immeasurably vast that only a little model of the solar system can even be depicting how the solar system really looks, because only God can see the actual little solar system as it actually exists.

Little Observatories

I visited the little Griffith Park Observatory, and,
saw what I thought didn't be anything
other than,
how the little solar system looks, and,
even got a little feeling
for how vastly separated
the little planets are
from each other.

Prologue to
Seven Wonders Of The World

This little poem contains a little information about the **New Seven Wonders Of The World** which were voted on as the new seven wonders of the world by a little internet vote of over a little hundred million little votes. Of the ancient seven wonders of the world, the only one still extant are the pyramids of Egypt. These new seven wonders, along with the pyramids of Egypt, would even be decent little vacation sites, for even viewing the little wonders of the world and even tasting the little culture of another little country.

Seven Wonders Of The World

Little me didn't even do anything other than
visit the seven newest wonders of the world.
First, I went to little Rio de Janeiro, Brazil,
and saw the 105-foot tall "Christ the Redeemer" statue.
Secondly, I visited little Rome, Italy,
and saw the little Colosseum.
Thirdly, I went to India,
and gazed on the Taj Mahal.
Fourthly, I even went to little China,
and walked on the Great Wall of China.
Fifthly, I visited Jordan,
and saw the ancient city of Petra.
Sixthly, I visited little Peru,
and visited the Inca ruins of Machu Picchu.
And lastly, I visited little Mexico,
and saw the ancient Maya city of Chichen Itza.

Prologue to
Why Curse?

This little poem calls to mind the commandment given to Moses by God in exodus 20:7, "Thou shalt not take the name of the Lord thy God in vain; for the Lord will not hold him guiltless that taketh his name in vain."

Why Curse?

I opened my little ignorant mouth
and out came little verbal garbage.
I sincerely believe that my little mouth
and my little tongue
were made to glorify the Lord.
And nothing other than saying,
why would I defile the little organs
that mention the name of the Lord
with vile and filthy language,
and then turn around
and use those same little lips
to supposedly glorify my Creator?
I think that if I use the same little mouth
to glorify the Lord
that I use for little profanity,
then, I'm taking the name of the Lord
in vain!!!!!

Prologue to
Stealing From The Lord

This little poem is very very clearly clear.

Stealing From The Lord

When I rob a little human being
of something that the Lord has blessed him with,
I'm stealing from the Lord!!!!!
We don't really own anything.
Everything we own, the Lord has blessed us with.
And when the Lord blesses us with anything,
we're only using it, for,
it really belongs to the Lord!!!!!
When we even earn our little possessions,
they're really little blessings from the Lord,
because the Lord blessed us
with the ability to earn those little possessions.
So, when I steal anything from any human being
I'm literally robbing the One who blessed
that little human being
with whatever I rob him of!!!!!

Prologue to
Little Borrowers

This little poem is even very clear.

Little Borrowers

The little borrowers
who refuse to pay back their borrowed whatever,
aren't anything other than,
robbing their little lender
of whatever they borrowed from him!!!!!
And little borrowing thieves
aren't anything other than,
stealing from the Lord!!!!!

Prologue to
Little Thieves

This little poem is a little very clear.

Little Thieves

When I purchase stolen property,
I'm just as much a little thief
as the one who stole the little property
that I supposedly purchased!!!!!
A little buyer of stolen anything
is really the little instigator
of the little actual theft,
nothing other than,
for the little reason of it being,
if the little actual thief
had no little buyer for his stolen little wares,
the little actual thief
wouldn't have any reason to steal,
other than,
for his own personal use,
and that's still a little thieving human being!!!!!

Prologue to
Little DVD And CD Thieves

Little this little poem isn't anything other than a little clear.

Little DVD And CD Thieves

The little DVD and CD thieves
sell little stolen movies
and little stolen songs,
for the little reason of it being,
they illegally copied
a valuable asset
of copyrighted material.
And so, if we buy little bogus DVDs
and little bogus CDs,
from a little thief,
we're a little thief our own little self!!!!!
Little thieves sitting in a little cell
aren't anything other than,
caught and prosecuted little thieves!!!!!
Little buyers of stolen anything
aren't anything other than,
little uncaught
and unprosecuted little thieves,
and even little uncaught
and unprosecuted little criminals!!!!!

Prologue to
Little Vending Machine Thieves

This little poem about little thieving human beings is as clear as our other little poems about little hidden thieves.

Little Vending Machine Thieves

When little so and so
put his money in the little vending machine,
little so and so asked me a little question,
namely, "How about a paper for yourself?"
When little me heard that little question,
little me even responded,
a little thusly,
"Little so and so,
if I want a little newspaper,
I'll take out my own money
and put it in the vending machine
and purchase my little newspaper,
rather than take a stolen little newspaper
that you're even offering me!!!!!"

Prologue to
The DUI Tests

This little poem is telling law enforcement that a certain little level of alcohol in the blood stream or a certain level of vaporized alcohol in the breath of a suspected drunk driver isn't any indication of even being a little intoxicated or even drunk, at least not necessarily.

The DUI Tests

When the officer tested my breath,
I wasn't nothing other than,
called a little drunk by the officer.
And when the officer said,
"Walk the little line, please.",
I walked the little line
straighter than the officer
could walk the little line.
So, when the officer
tested by little body
in other little ways,
I passed every little test!!!!!
So, when I went to the little court,
the only little evidence
against me was a little
breath test result, and,
the faulty memory
of the little arresting officer!!!!!

Prologue to
The Little Blood Test

This little poem isn't anything other than asking little society a very simple little question.

The Little Blood Test

The little blood test
isn't anything other than saying,
"There is a certain amount of alcohol
in a certain little blood stream."
Little ignorant little blood test
can't give out any information
about the condition
of the consciousness
of any human being.
The little blood test
isn't any indication of anything
other than,
the blood alcohol level
is a little such and such.
I once drank fifteen little beers
in a little eight hours or so,
and I wasn't even intoxicated,
but I'll bet
my little blood alcohol level
was way over the little legal limit!!!!!

Prologue to
Three Little Strikes

This little poem is trying to tell little lawmakers that a little ignorant little law that calls a human being nothing other than a habitual criminal if he commits three little felonies is nothing other than the most ignorant little law that any little ignorant little legislative body can even ever put into the little law books!!!!!

Three Little Strikes

Little me stole a little piece of pizza,
and it was my third little felony conviction,
so the judge gave me
a little twenty-five years to life
for a third little strike.
Little my little cellmate
didn't nothing other than
kill a little human being,
and made a little deal,
and he got a little ten little years!!!!!

Prologue to
The Real Lawmaker

This little poem doesn't even be anything other than saying that little legislatures aren't nothing other than inspired and sometimes Willed by the Highest Being That Exists to make laws that conform to His purpose for even creating little human beings. And nothing other than saying, the little purpose of the Creator creating little human beings isn't any little reason other than for the little human beings to even be maturing into more mature human beings. So, consequently, the Creator sometimes Wills little legislatures to pass a little ignorantly ignorant little law that He even wants them to even be looking at after they pass it so they can mature a little bit by recognizing how ignorantly ignorant that little law is that they just passed. So the Creator tests the little maturity of the little legislature by even Willing them to even look at the little law they just passed to see if it's a just little law. If they decide it's a just little law, the Creator even lets it go into effect so that the little citizens can even recognize its little ignorantly ignorant ignorance and even get involved in the little democratic process to cause the legislature to change that ignorantly ignorant little law, thereby becoming more mature little human beings.

The Real Lawmaker

The Creator inspires legislatures
to pass His little laws
other than,
when He tests little legislatures
by various little methods.
He even tests little citizens
by passing ignorant little laws
for causing little citizens
to even get involved
in the democratic process.
The little legislatures aren't nothing other than,
the little instruments of the Creator
for making His little secular laws.

Prologue to
Little Finality

This little poem isn't anything other than summing up all of the little poems of this little book in one final little poem.

Little Finality

The end of ignorant behavior
isn't nothing other than,
the little beginning
of the Kingdom of God on earth!!!!!
Jesus said,
the Kingdom is within.
So, when little human beings
rid themselves of little ignorant behavior
and start manifesting
the Kingdom within,
then the Kingdom will even be a reality
in the little outward existences, and,
the Kingdom of God on earth will finally exist!!!!!

Prologue to
THE KINGDOM OF GOD

This little poem doesn't nothing other than give a little glimpse of a little future society where the little admonitions and the little advices and the little precepts and the little commandments and even the little everything given to the prophets and the gurus and the messengers of the Highest Being That Exists aren't anything other than followed by even every little human being.

THE KINGDOM OF GOD

The little future society isn't anything other than,
Heading into an even higher society
Even than the little immediate future society.

Kings will envy even an average human being
In the little even immediate future society,
Nothing other than saying,
Getting out of the present little evilest little society
Doesn't even be anything other than
Our little duty as little believers in
Many of the prophets and gurus and messengers.

Our little duty isn't any little
Fondest idle fancy.

God isn't even nothing other than,
Only the propelling Force
Directing society into the Kingdom of God on earth.

Epilogue

When I wrote this little book, I didn't intend it to even be anything other than for my own little personal use as a little collection of little poems that I had composed over my little lifetime that I even shared with several little friends and acquaintances. Howbeit,, the little book is so universally oriented that I even decided to publish it and even share it with as many people as I could because it contains very important information about certain little things that many human beings aren't even aware of that might even help those human beings avoid little devastating little calamities in their little lives, so, here is my little contribution to what I hope will make this a better little world.

www.ingramcontent.com/pod-product-compliance
Lightning Source LLC
Chambersburg PA
CBHW021058080526
44587CB00010B/291